Mending a Wounded LIFE

Gentle Words for Healing

Brenda Grey

Published by
Creative Bound Inc.
P.O. Box 424,
Carp, Ontario
Canada K0A 1L0
(613) 831-3641

ISBN 0-921165-44-7
Printed and bound in Canada

Cover design by Rob Grey
Text design and formatting by Wendelina O'Keefe

Canadian Cataloguing in Publication Data

Grey, Brenda
Mending a wounded life : gentle words for healing

ISBN 0-921165-44-7

1. Healing. 2. Meditation. 3. Self-actualization (Psychology). I. Title.

BT732.5.G74 1996 158'.12 C96-900081-2

Acknowledgments

I would like to send my warmest gratitude to all of my teachers, friends, advisors and those who taught me the way to understand, help, and share love.

I am grateful to Dr. Tadeusz Grygier, my dear friend whom I respect deeply, for helping me to understand the complexity of human behavior. Tad, I thank you for all that you have done for humanity.

To Gail Pike, my publisher, for seeing the need to help people, and believing as I do in the healing power of love.

Special thanks to my husband Rob, whom with deep conviction and creativity designed the most beautiful cover for my book.

Dedication

I dedicate this book to my husband Rob, and my three wonderful children, Jamie, Julie and Jansen. I hope that all of you continuously grow in truth and love throughout your lives.

Contents

Introduction

This book is dedicated to those who wish to help themselves heal and find fulfilment in their lives. All we really need in order to do this is the sincere desire to be happy, and life will be transformed from sorrow to a joyous celebration.

Life is not meant to be full of pain and struggle. We are meant to live lovingly, and that comes about when we earnestly desire to do so. We cannot find peace until we stop bombarding ourselves with negative, conflicting messages, for such messages are only second-hand knowledge, and they cause defeatist and subservient thinking. We can eliminate doubt, fear and resentment from our lives by recognizing that they are controlling, destructive influences. Once we become aware of this, we can go on to change the way we think, so that negative thinking becomes unnecessary. Life then becomes broader, full of opportunity and fulfilment. We can live life lovingly, rather than being guided by unhappy circumstances.

When we let go of distorted thinking and listen to inner lessons of understanding and acceptance, we begin to see life in a more enriched way. We then can choose autonomy, which allows us the freedom to believe in ourselves. We make our dreams come true and learn to live life to its fullest. Most of all, we come to excel in our uniqueness and find peace within ourselves. We finally do what is right for us; we do what brings us inner satisfaction and love.

This book sets out simple, step-by-step techniques that will guide the reader along the journey of healing. Practice and patience are important in the transition to healing, but most significantly you have to believe in your own inner beauty.

The power of love

We are eternally connected to the spiritual, healing energy of love. At times, the pain we have experienced prevents us from accepting this connection, because it is hard to believe in anything when we are suffering.

We cannot change what we have gone through, but we can change our present circumstances and state of mind. Once we accept and believe in the power of love, healing takes place. First, it comes to us in glimpses, wanting us to see the meaning of our life. Regrettably, at times we only respond when we are so far down that it becomes our last resort. When we do respond, our pain slowly subsides, because we finally understand that our life is an experience we choose and from which we need to learn.

Our purpose is to forgive, love, share and live. Once we accept the healing power of love, we extend this love to others, thereby extending love's healing power. Once we acknowledge that our gift is love, we accept, believe and learn to trust ourselves and others.

Healing our wounded hearts

All healing takes time, patience and work. First of all, start with the desire to change the discord that is in your life. Then, with trust and commitment to be liberated, your life can become a place of comfort, rather than one of pain, anger and confusion.

It takes a great deal of patience with the process, and trust in yourself. Be willing to be honest and to share your feelings and thoughts; be willing to feel what needs to be felt. Most of all, do not be afraid, for nothing will be any worse or more difficult to bear than it is right now; little by little, the changes are felt.

Nothing that is worth achieving comes from a quick fix. It takes time to heal and mend a wounded heart. It takes love, forgiveness and effort to change from the old to the new. It takes time to see the results and reap the benefits, but it is well worth it.

We are more than is apparent to our eyes alone; we are the embodiment of a peaceful self that has been hidden because of our negative experiences. When we open our minds and are willing to listen to the profound messages of truth that try to reach us, we unlock secret treasures within. Healing takes place when we choose to heal and to be at peace with ourselves, with others and with our past, so that a new beginning can take place.

Taking the first step

Taking the first step toward healing seems difficult, but once we are willing to take it we start the process of cleansing ourselves, and healing does take place. The first step is cleansing ourselves from anger and pain using our own internal resource of love.

Anger that is not dealt with is like a volcano that is always waiting to erupt. It is affecting us even at this very moment unless it is resolved. This anger can be carried over to our everyday relationships, sometimes destroying what is most important to us.

Unless we heal, all the emotions that evoke our reactions can be projected on to every facet of our lives and on to every person with whom we come in contact. In order to heal, we have to learn to forgive. We have repressed our anger for so long that we feel guilty when the memories come back. Accepting that they are only memories, and that they cannot harm us now, is part of our battle. Cleansing ourselves and learning to love is part of our reward.

Our life is like a puzzle—all the pieces must be put in place before the picture is complete. Once the puzzle is in place, we are then committed to making all our dreams become our reality. We recognize real beauty and love, and seek to integrate them into our lives. We walk with life, instead of ten steps behind it.

We suddenly experience a longing to surround ourselves with healthy relationships and positive experiences. We become aware that forgiving and accepting will be part of our reward, and with that comes a new realization that when we forgive we are allowing the blessings of life to be received.

Forgiveness heals. It is something that comes not from a medicine cabinet, but from our hearts. It cures many ills that deny us freedom and happiness. Choose to heal, and love will bring freedom and happiness.

Taking charge of your life and healing

A human life is like a story that unfolds as it moves from birth to death.

You are the editor of your own story. If your story is full of anger, hurt and disappointment, you can change how your story reads by changing how you view it.

Think of your life before you as a diary and your mind as recording the information. Your reactions become confused when you observe memories of you filled with unresolved anger and blaming. As the editor, you can change the story so that it is light and easy reading.

Remember, everything we *think* happens inside us, not outside; change the pattern of thinking and your world will change.

Healing takes place when we accept that everything we have experienced helps us to learn and grow stronger. The more difficult the experience, the more enlightened we become, providing we make an effort to understand the meaning.

It all sounds so difficult, but it is not; it just takes patience and belief in your own self. It takes the desire to be happy and have what you want in life, and it takes trust. There is no one controlling your thoughts except you; there is no one controlling your destiny or your happiness except you. Once this fact is accepted, control is no longer displaced. You realize that taking charge of your life means renouncing all that has controlled your happiness.

Dependency and rage go hand-in-hand

Learned helplessness and loss of self-esteem derive from an inability to love ourselves. We turn outward and sometimes find faulty relationships to fill the emptiness that continually haunts us. Various relationships may temporarily fill the void for a while, until disappointment and rage can no longer be repressed and escalate to reinforce our inadequacy and powerlessness. Depending on others to fill us with love when we are not complete will only cause perpetual dependency, instead of positive mutual dependency.

Meditations

The meditations in this book are a means of creating a positive self-image. Meditation is also a way of taking charge, focusing on new and positive thoughts, and replacing old ones. To make meditation easier, relax by practising slow, deep breathing. Feel the relaxation flow to every part of your body. This should be done when seated comfortably in a quiet room with no distractions. Soft music also helps by lowering the body's energy level.

Your thoughts can be changed to a kaleidoscope of great enlightenment if they are reprogrammed through acceptance, forgiveness and understanding. Remember, anything repeated enough becomes mastered. Be patient with the process, and trust your ability. Most of all, learn to love yourself, for this is your gift in life.

Happiness

Happiness is our blessing if we commit ourselves to work out our pain and heal. Yesterday brought experiences we did not choose. Some of them left us confused, unhappy and in darkness. Sometimes they took away our innocence. We can regain that joyous innocence if we accept the responsibility for healing. Claiming dignity and freedom is our right. Loving ourselves is our responsibility to God. Discovering inner peace and joy is what we owe to ourselves.

Meditation

Today I choose to see only the positive side of my life, the one I am creating for myself. I want a newly found happiness that is my right, and I will be open to learn the right way of living.

Loneliness

Emotionally starved adults do whatever is needed to cover up their loneliness. Loneliness is a feeling that there is no one there for us that we can turn to and with whom we can be deeply connected. An inability to connect to another human being leaves us feeling a desperate need that, for a while, may be suppressed with drugs, sex, alcohol or food. We ignore signals that continuously trigger messages we refuse to heed, and so we sink deeper into a quagmire of detachment and fear from what we need the most—love and closeness with another.

Meditation

Try for just one moment to be honest with yourself. Admit that you are unable to cope with the inner pain that is causing your loneliness. Admit that loving someone, and being loved, would be much more satisfactory than using means of escape that cause deep shame and sorrow.

Repeat,

I do need someone to turn to and rely on instead of using negative alternatives that hurt me more. In time as I heal, I will have that special person to share my life with.

Willingness to take the steps

The second step may be different for everyone. It might be letting the pain surface slowly, it might mean crying or remembering, or releasing and letting go. It may be feeling repressed anger, or dealing with unwarranted shame. It will almost certainly be difficult at first, but do not give up. Trust that in time you will be freed from a life of unhappiness. The desire to be happy will lead you there!

Meditation

Admit to your self that you want to be free of the hurt and anger with which you have lived. If anger interferes with your desire to heal, remember, you are making the choice to be happy and free. You are now taking the second step to be in control of your life! Believe that it will work!

Repeat,

I want to be happy, I want to be at peace, I will do what it takes to be whom I choose to be.

Love starts inside

Love is not something we have to seek, because it already dwells within our hearts. Our passion and need for love is the evidence of love that we have not yet discovered. The love we feel for others is the love we must give first to ourselves before we can share healthy loving relationships. We must first accept our own selves, lovingly, before we can offer love to anyone else in a healthy way. We must want others to treat us the way we deserve to be treated. Love is KIND and FAIR, and that is how our lives should be. Love multiplies as it flows. To share love and to give it we must experience the completeness of love. Love is also knowing the importance of others as we know our own importance. Love does not seek to gain from the recipient, for it has fulfilled itself by giving. Love's genuine purpose is to multiply and bring joy. Just as time and eternity are inseparable, so are love and life.

Meditation

Sit quietly and focus on someone or something you love (make sure the object of your love brings no painful memories). Let the love you are now feeling slowly flow from your thoughts through the rest of your body, warming, healing and strengthening as it goes.

It is very important that we claim this love as ours, and do not let it escape our physical and psychological being. This love must be claimed as ours first before it can be given to anyone else.

Expressing and releasing

At times, we overreact to circumstances and we are unaware of the source of our reactions. Our unconscious mind is trying to release pent-up anger, asking us to work it out properly. No one is born angry, and no one is meant to live with anger. This is not what life is about. Going back and working on the issues that caused the anger will allow us to live harmoniously in the present. Placing past anger where it belongs, allows us to function calmly and effectively in the present.

Meditation

It is important that you be with someone whom you trust and who is understanding. Ask the person not to say anything, just to listen. It must be done freely and honestly. Calm your mind before you start to express your feelings. Go only as far as you are able to at this time. If you have to scream or cry, go ahead, but remember that if you do, it will start the healing process. Try to deal with one issue at a time, for this eliminates confusion, so that each issue that has hurt you will be dealt with completely. It will be overwhelming at first, but over time the results will be remarkable.

Life is meant to move forward

We may be unaware that we are being controlled by hurt and fear. If so, we cannot allow the beauty of love to come into our life. Fear is a crippling mechanism that paralyses us and prevents us from being close to anyone. Fear is a trap that keeps us immobile. We can only go as far back and forward as that trap will allow us to move.

Life is meant to move forward. It is progression and learning, which lead us to understanding and freedom. We are here in order to learn to overcome the imperfections in life, not to claim them as part of our being. We are here not to dwell on failures and hurts, but to celebrate life and our accomplishments.

Meditation

It is very important that you fill your mind with a memory that has made you feel deep inner love. (The love is what you must feel, not the object of the love itself.) Hold this memory as a shield, while you "watch" an unhappy thought. The person that caused the unhappiness cannot hurt you now, because you are protected by love. The shield of love is stronger than the disturbing memory.

Surround yourself with love

There have been many people with whom we have shared our time and lives; some have made a positive impact, others a negative one. Remember the positive experiences and how wonderful they felt. These positive encounters might only have lasted a fleeting moment, but focus on the warmth and love that flowed so freely at that time. Seek to surround yourself with relationships like these while you are healing.

Meditation

Affirm that you were created perfect. See yourself surrounded by all of those wonderful people who have come into your life, and feel the power of their love as it heals you. Even if they were just passers-by, remember the moment and the warmth you felt as you were touched by them.

Letting go

Dwelling on a problem creates confusion and frustration. When a crisis occurs, remember that the solution will arise within you. Do not focus on the problem, feeling helpless. Look for the answer, and it will come. Trust in your own wisdom, and affirm that truth will guide you to the result you wish to achieve.

Meditation

Confirm quietly that the solution already lies within yourself. Although you are in the midst of turmoil, nothing can destroy your sense of calm. Hold on to that thought, and feel the delight of knowing that you are guided in all you do.

Fill yourself with illumination

Unresolved hurts and disappointments are affecting us even now, at this very moment. We become illuminated with understanding and forgiveness when we let go of hate. It's hard, but do not give in to bitterness; it has a profound and negative affect on our well-being. Life is a gift of joy, and it is our right to be happy. Be willing to receive the gift of life.

Meditation

Slowly and thoughtfully, visualize each person who has hurt you; hear them asking for your forgiveness. Forgive them, and feel the release of pain; admit aloud that you will forgive them, for they made mistakes. We must try to learn from everything life teaches us, but most of all we must remember that to gain understanding is to become a richer person. Remember, forgiving means letting go of the anger within yourself. It does not mean you have to be in communion with that person if you do not wish to be.

Believe in the power of healing

Believe in the healing process. There will be times when new emotions emerge and you may become frightened. Let yourself experience these emotions; they are just part of what has been repressed. Real happiness comes from healing. There is a newly found joy that emerges, grows and fills your heart, until one day it becomes the total energy force in your life. When this happens, all sorrow will leave you.

Meditation

Think about the happiest moment in your life. It may have been a walk on a beach, or the smile of an innocent child. Concentrate totally on the joy you felt. Acknowledge that this is what you seek to have in your heart all the time, and it will be given to you.

We can change our attitudes

Most of our attitudes have been molded by our past experiences and, of course, our own reactions to these experiences. When we are violated and disappointed by people we have trusted, it causes us perpetual mistrust. It affects our judgment to the point that we find it difficult to trust even ourselves. Unfortunately, a flicker of anger lives inside us where there should be a flame of love. Sadly, we hurt our own selves and miss the beauty that life has to offer, unless we really want to make a change in our lives. Changing things is not really difficult; it takes only practice and a few positive experiences to prove it can happen.

Meditation

Every morning, when you get out of bed, say out loud to yourself,

I forgive myself for all I have done; the past cannot punish me.

A new attitude can be yours

Up to now, your mind has been programmed by past experiences. This does not have to be, especially if they have been unhealthy experiences. Affirm now that every new experience is a new beginning. Look at every person with a fresh attitude, and you will attract new friends and experiences.

Meditation

If there is something you would like to experience, close your eyes and imagine it happening. Feel the totality of the experience, and believe that all you have to do is desire it enough and it will happen.

Opportunities are there for the taking

We prevent ourselves from seeing vast opportunities because we see ourselves as incapable. If we give precedence to this false belief, we miss out on our creative abilities. We can choose to believe that we are incapable of being any more than we are, or we can tap into our inner connection to God's love. Once we are connected to this love, we feel its vastness and lean on the strength it gives us to expand to be all we wish to be.

Meditation

In the quietness of your mind, still all thoughts and calmly focus on the word "life" ... now focus on the word "myself." Think about all the beauty in life and see the word "self" connected to that beauty. The word "my" is the element of free will that has been given to you to express your right to happiness. You are the co-creator of your life, and the Creator has given you the right to live lovingly and joyously. This means creating your own opportunities.

You are in control

Until now, we have been the sum total of the progression of our experiences and ideas. We can change this progression, make it positive instead of negative, by evaluating each thought and idea. If the idea has been conducive to harmonious thinking, then claim it; if not, let it go and see a positive outcome instead of holding on to something that has no relevancy in your life at this moment. Reaffirm positive thoughts about yourself, instead of negative ones.

Meditation

See yourself as an open tunnel. You have control over the energy that flows through it. Fill your mind with good thoughts and ideas, accepting the fact that there is no room for negative thoughts in a peaceful mind. The more you practice this belief, the more it will become your reality.

The sun always shines

Never allow doubt to enter your mind during your transition to healing. A flower does not stop blooming because it doubts the sun will shine. Everyday it lives for nourishment, expanding and growing more beautiful. The progression of healing is like a flower: First the seed is planted and the roots grow in fertile ground. Then its petals and leaves develop so that it can share its beauty with the world.

Meditation

See your inner self growing and developing, so that every part of your body is healing and joyful. Look inside, and trust in your self; believe without questioning that you are growing, changing and learning a new way of life.

Without faith in yourself there is nothing

Faith is total belief in yourself. When you were a child you felt you could do almost anything, the only thing that was an obstacle was your dependence on others, either for approval or for support. If you were fortunate enough to have the means to reach your goals, then you did; if not, then you didn't. Now that you are an adult, you do not need the approval of others. All you need to succeed is the desire, dedication and total belief in your own abilities.

Meditation

Your inner self is as pure as a child, full of joy and love for life. You are now responsible for giving life to your innermost desires. Thoughtfully and carefully, focus on what you desire with a faithful, committed belief that it will come true.

Dreams do come true

Never give up on your dreams. Affirm that your dreams are your desires and aspirations. Focus with total commitment on each dream, seeing yourself as part of it. If a negative thought tries to make you see the opposite of what you want, stop it immediately and refocus on the dream.

Meditation

The power of the universe dwells in your inner self. Focus on the positive self that governs your life. Participate in the dream, visualize it clearly, and watch it unfold over time.

Life can change if you believe in yourself

Your thoughts and desires have guided you to where you are at this point in your life. Change your thought patterns from fearful doubts to positive thinking, and you will change your life.

Meditation

Dreams have a beginning and an ending. The beginning is in our minds. The ending is when we give life to our dreams. Accept this fact with your whole heart, and make it come true by focusing all of your energy into a positive, non-doubting mode.

Learning to love yourself

Be true to yourself; do not be ashamed of who you are. All that has happened to make you feel ashamed or guilty was beyond your control, or it would never have happened. Now that you are in the present, let yourself be free to know your strengths; seek to know yourself and you will also know others. Forgiving is part of learning to love yourself, because if you do not forgive, the chains of fear, anger and guilt will destroy your ability to grow and to understand.

You are on a journey of self-discovery leading to freedom. You are on the road to healing, and part of that healing is learning to love yourself. Loving yourself bears no conditions that demand you be perfect. The only condition love imposes is that you faithfully and freely give it to yourself, so you can truly share it with others. It is your right to love yourself just because you have life, no strings attached. (It is not your right that others love you, for they have their own journey to understanding what love is.)

Meditation

Be true to yourself, and break out of the chains

that hold you trapped. Be true to yourself, and always accept the fact that, at the time, you did the best you were able to do.

Nothing can change the past, but you can change the future. See the future as a place where your new love for yourself will guide you and bring you the special things in life that you deserve.

The Kingdom of Heaven is within

Heaven and hell reside in us. We decide whether we shall go through the door to heaven within, or remain in our own hell. Heaven is ours for the asking, and when we listen to its inspirational guidance it takes us gently on a journey that protects us from all the negative energy with which we have lived for so long. The Kingdom of Heaven is on earth, within us all.

Meditation

Focus on loving feelings that flow from your heart. Let them circle back into your body and feel their healing power. If a negative thought interrupts the flow, let the flow of love wash it away, and continue the circle of love flowing through you and back to you.

Anger does not belong to you

When anger creeps into your mind, send it away. You are in control of your feelings and your inner world. Affirm this and believe this. Anger distorts your thoughts, limits your mental abilities, and deprives you of your energy. Look carefully at the hostility you feel within, and know that you truly do not want to be connected to it.

Meditation

Calmly state,

I am free of all negative forces; they can not penetrate my being, because I am love, harmony and peace. Anger is separate from me, and cannot harm me.

Nothing that exists beyond love and peace belongs to you.

Repeat,

I am filled with peaceful thoughts, and they belong to me.

Dwelling in peace

Peace dwells deep in our hearts. Unfortunately, we have not recognized the sanctuary within, because we have raised barriers in order to protect ourselves. But barriers do not remove obstacles. They are merely a defence mechanism that, in turn, creates more obstacles and more problems. They limit our ability to trust, to give and to forgive. In other words, barriers prevent us from experiencing unconditional love. Let go of one defence mechanism just for a moment; the result will be that you will begin to connect to your own inner source of peace.

Meditation

Deep in your heart, beyond the defence mechanisms you have created, there is a place that is harmonious. Nothing can harm you there; you are at one with this harmonious peaceful self. Love fills you with comfort. You are loved.

How do you see the world?

Your inner feelings and beliefs determine how you see the outer world. Compare your observations and opinions about this world with how you feel inside. They correlate. Your outer expressions are what you feel and think inside. They are unacknowledged inner feelings expressed outwardly to the world. If you see the world as an unhappy place, it is your own unhappiness that you are projecting outward.

Meditation

See yourself as fair, kind and loving. Give first to yourself, unconditionally, and you will give to others in the same way. There is nothing *outside* your self that can affect your love *for* your self.

We are now grown up

When we were children we had no defences against those who chose to hurt us. Now that we are adults, we are responsible for our own happiness and our own safety. No one can harm those who truly love themselves, because such persons seek only loving experiences, and if they are confronted with uncomfortable situations, they view them with understanding, instead of with feelings of helplessness.

Meditation

You are encompassed with a shield of love; let it radiate from within your heart, through your body and mind. Feel its protecting, golden radiance. Walk gently protected by the armor of love for yourself, and it will protect you against all hurt.

Seek healthy relationships

Our feelings of being attracted to new people can be distorted by negative past relationships. There have been times when many of us have been overwhelmed and drawn to a certain type of person. We might even have mistaken this attraction for love. Unless the relationships we form with others are healthy and allow us to grow and learn more about ourselves, then it is best to avoid relationships with certain people while we are healing.

Meditation

Close your eyes and see loving people surrounding you and sending kind, loving messages to you. Let their love embrace you, and let their trusting qualities guide you to your own true self.

Give to yourself first

We must first give love to ourselves and then, when we give it to others, there is a delightful inner reward. If we give to others and ignore our own needs, we risk resenting the recipients of our giving. Once we recognize our own needs, and ask gently that they be satisfied, then we give freely.

Meditation

In the quietness of your mind accept that everyone gives uniquely and can only give what they are capable of giving. Interpreting what they don't give as selfishness causes conflict between the giver and receiver. Accept all giving with a deep belief that everyone gives all that they can at any one time.

Believe in your dreams

We have all been given a special gift that is waiting to express its creativity through us. The passion we feel for our dreams is evidence of our own desire to share this creativity. Believe in your dreams with heartfelt conviction, and make them come true. The only difference between brilliance and mediocrity is dedication.

Meditation

Spend time every day focusing on an idea you wish to express. No matter if it is art, business or a hobby you love, see the finished product, and see yourself giving form and substance—even life—to your idea.

Understand your feelings

Everyone has suffered an injustice at some time in their life. The loss of a loved one, abuse or rejection may have caused pain in our life, and this fact has to be resolved. The mind wants the pain taken away, so we turn to outside sources to relieve our aching hearts and discover that these sources provide only temporary solutions. Learning to understand our feelings does away with the need to hide from the problem. All that we have endured can be turned into strength and fortitude instead of bitterness.

Meditation

In a dimly lit room, make yourself comfortable and breathe deeply until you feel relaxed. Repeat these words over and over again,

I see the person (use their name) *who has caused me this pain. I understand that at that time, he/she had no control over his/her actions. It was not my fault, therefore I am set free from the pain it has caused me.*

Relax a moment and then say,

I now see the story differently. I have no attachment, nor any need to hold on to the past, because I am now free of the anger that bound me to it.

Your thoughts belong to you

Your life belongs to you and you have the right to happiness! The only thing standing in your way is your perception of what you have endured. It is not the experience, but how you dealt with it, that hurt you. Change your perception to understanding and you will be free from the anger that has prevented you from being happy. Nothing that has ever happened to you can prevent you from healing. Nothing can destroy the power of love you hold within yourself, if you hold on to that love. Believe, and you will realize your deepest dreams.

Meditation

There is no magic formula, except to eliminate doubt, anger and fear, and see through the eyes of understanding and love.

Repeat,

I am in control of my thoughts, they are mine, so it is my right to control what I think and do.

Clinging to the past

Clinging to old, painful experiences can only hurt us. It is like tying a noose around our neck. It even feels the same, for when the pain emerges it chokes us to think about it, unless anger and guilt are released and replaced by love. It is not our place to punish ourselves for something that is no longer appropriate.

Meditation

It is difficult to let go of anger unless we ask our higher power within to help us. Love is God's energy that replaces anger and hate. Letting go without the help of God can leave us confused and empty.

Repeat,

I need God, Who is within, to help me release all anger that is holding me back. I trust and believe that all things are possible with God's help.

Forgiving

Forgiving blesses those who forgive and those who are forgiven.

Forgiving frees our heart from the chains of contempt. We harm ourselves the most when we hold someone in contempt, for contempt is a self-made prison. We incarcerate our thoughts to the point of confusion. We hold on to a time that has passed, and make it our present. It is over, it is done. By not letting it go, we give it power and attach it to our thoughts, thereby giving it control.

Meditation

Take each unforgiving thought, one at a time, and watch it. Examine the emotions and thoughts that control you and cling to you. Do not be afraid to feel the hurt and then express how you feel, as if it were happening. Ask God to help you. Eventually, as you do this, you will understand and forgive.

Unresolved hurt perpetuates anger

It is a burden to live with anger when life is meant to be a celebration of knowing and understanding. Anger must be released before healing can transform misery into joy. Tears are a means of cleansing anger and pain from the mind and body. Once we are brave enough to allow ourselves the freedom to weep, we wash away the anguish that has been torturing us.

Meditation

When your heart asks to be released from pain, then give it that release by cleansing yourself with tears. Let them flow until peace and calm wash over you. Eventually, peace will replace the pain forever.

Living inside

Sometimes we become "separated" from our body when we think it has betrayed us. We regard it as our enemy because of the pain it causes us if we do not forgive. Our body is the house of our soul, and we must trust it so that we can live peacefully within.

Meditation

Go deep inside and observe how comfortable you can feel within. Let go and empty all feelings and ideas that separate you from your body. Calm your mind and body by easing the tension away, starting at the top of your head and letting the feeling of relaxation flow through your body, right down to the tips of your toes. Stay inside, and enjoy the harmony you feel. Hold that feeling and walk to a full-length mirror; look at your reflection while maintaining the calm you feel. This way you can begin to harmonize your body and mind. Smile, look deeply into your own eyes, and let yourself feel only the unity of your mind and body.

Get in touch

If living in the present is filled with frustration, you may be living with displaced anger. Many times we project our emotional turmoil outward against those closest to us, without realizing where the anger really belongs.

If this is so, maybe it is time to be honest with ourselves and place the anger where it belongs. We have the right to be angry when we have been violated and abandoned. We have the right to express our disappointment at those who have neglected our needs. We also have the right to stay away from those who continue to hurt us intentionally. Sometimes, we even have to leave those people whom we love until they change.

Meditation

The next time you feel overwhelmed by displaced anger, turn back for a moment and see if it is connected to an incident in your life that has not been worked out. Once you see where the anger belongs, quietly "observe" the feelings you experience and resolve the problem at hand. Now the problem cannot hurt you any longer, for it belongs in the past.

Inferiority complexes can be changed

Inferiority complexes stem from doubt and lack of love for ourselves. Once we realize who we really are, there is no room for one drop of doubt. Once we realize that all strength and fortitude belong to us, then the masks we have worn in the past are stripped away and we gain complete confidence in ourselves.

Meditation

See yourself connected to the light of God; you are God's creation. What God creates is perfect. Choose God's creation, not the imperfections that you have created from shame, guilt and anger.

The voice within

Living in conflict and confusion causes us to miss the messages we receive from our inner selves. Sometimes, messages are referred to as intuition, or our higher power. The voice within is God's loving guidance. Listen to the truth that is spoken; it seeks to guide us in the right direction, leading away from our pain and confusion; it seeks to eliminate all conflict and insecurity.

Meditation

Quietly go inward and calm your mind. Listen to the river of knowledge that flows through you. Let this message of loving knowledge be your guide.

Repeat,

I will let go of anger and doubt. I will listen to the truth that is within.

Journey

Life is meant to be a journey to selfhood that brings fulfilment, peace and joy. These only come when there is a total surrender of old beliefs. This opens the door to a perfect union with your inner strength, guiding you on your journey to a new way of living.

Meditation

Accept the fact that God dwells in your heart. Your responsibility is to attain oneness with this strength. All that is positive, loving and true is of God. Seek to know the personal connection you have to God, and miracles will be yours.

Resentments

Sometimes things we are not aware of cause us distress. Our unconscious resentments and the grudges we hold against others can cause all kinds of illnesses if not dealt with. It is only ourselves we harm by not forgiving and by not living in a loving way.

The energy we waste on resenting other peoples' mistakes is not conducive to peace of mind. We are capable of protecting ourselves now. We are no longer defenceless.

Meditation

Go deep inside and be still. Seek out what is holding you back from living in a loving way. Say out loud,

I release myself from all resentments that are preventing my happiness.

It is never too late...

Choose today to seek inner peace and watch the remarkable results. This does not mean compromising, but understanding yourself and others.

Condemnation does not bring peace, nor does unresolved anger. Understand that the situations that have hurt you were beyond your control, or otherwise they would never have happened. You are now capable of making the decision to keep away from destructive relationships. You are now free to live lovingly and share that love with healthy people.

Meditation

Today, choose to listen with a non-judgmental mind. Today, choose to see through a peaceful mind, for you seek peaceful thoughts.

Responsibility

It is no longer your responsibility to blame yourself or others. The past does not exist anymore, except in the form of the negative thoughts that lay claim to you at this moment. You are no longer responsible for the source of the anger that has caused you so much pain. Your responsibility is to be forgiving and at peace. Understanding opens the gate to forgiving the tortured souls who have caused you harm. No one can inflict any degree of pain on another, unless they have experienced the same degree of pain at the hands of others.

Meditation

Affirm the following:

I am willing to take responsibility for forgiving myself and others.

I no longer want to claim the anger that is affecting my peace of mind at this moment.

Keep centered

Make it your goal in life to heal, and everything else will unfold the way you desire. There is no longer reason to allow the past to damage your future. It is your right to be happy and have all that brings you peace and joy. Keep centered on your inner convictions and source of love. If you give life to love, none of your past troubles will have power over your newly found joy.

Meditation

A wonderful meditation to repeat several times a day while in the transition of healing:

I am committed to heal, and no longer see myself as a victim but as a person who now has the opportunity to grow and be happy. I am committed to releasing myself from any abusive situations that are victimizing me.

All problems have solutions

Acknowledge that there are solutions to all problems. Dwelling on problems causes unnecessary stressful thinking and confusion. When we change our thought pattern to finding solutions we eliminate anxiety and enrich our power to be better problem solvers. Strive to be a finder of solutions instead of a dweller on problems.

Meditation

For today, think about one solution that is waiting to be discovered in your mind. This may be a solution to a personal problem or a circumstance beyond your control. Focus only on your desire to see the answer, not on the negative aspects of the problem itself. Find strength within. The more you concentrate on the solution, the quicker the problem vanishes.

Do not give power to falsehood

Validating our faults or shortcomings is one cause of depression and anger that affect our feeling of self-worth. Maybe you were once told you were inadequate, and you fixed this false idea in your memory, thus preventing belief in your true abilities. Doing this only serves to give power to falsehood.

Meditation

You are a creation of God's image, and you are perfect in the eyes of God. It is only you who believes otherwise.

Repeat,

I have been created perfectly in God's image, it is only me who sees otherwise. Therefore, I am now committed to seeing myself as the God-created me—good, forgiven and at peace.

Everything starts with an idea

Everything that exists begins as an idea. The house you build, the business you run, all start as an idea. The life you choose to live is the life created by you. No one who ever accomplished anything worthwhile ever gave up.

Meditation

Everything is first created in our minds. Fill your mind with ideas you wish to make real. Persist with them to the end, until they are accomplished, and your creative energies will bring you the rewards that come with completion.

No one controls your thoughts

Only you control your thoughts. Holding on to negative, painful thoughts gives life to a confusing and conflicting waste of energy. You can renounce all negative thoughts. Seek to think in an enriched and positive way. Loving yourself is positive, claiming empowerment is positive.

Meditation

Understanding and acceptance are what you strive for, so choose to have control over how you think.

Affirm,

Today I will try to understand myself and others rather than letting negative thoughts control me.

Acceptance of who we are

The feeling that we are unworthy reflects our lack of acceptance of who we really are. This feeling also affects our ability to renew our aspirations. Learning, growing and believing in who we are encourages us to find new opportunities and challenges. Everyone is meant to find their own inherent gifts and realize their dreams. Everyone is meant to develop the riches hidden deep within.

Meditation

Repeat several times,
I trust in myself. I am worthy of all the greatness life has to offer. I thank God for all that is and all that will be.

Singular autonomy

We all want to have power over the way we live and over our destiny. This is quite simple to achieve once we realize that we are in charge of the direction we take so as to live truthfully and peacefully with ourselves. Creating a mental image of what we wish for, and diligently holding on to that image, brings us closer to our dreams. Developing a way of expressing our uniqueness in a constructive way brings life to our dreams.

Meditation

Affirm,

God's power and love guide me to all that is good and right. I am filled with all that is needed to make my dreams come true.

Trust in your beliefs

If your beliefs lie in hoping for your own betterment and the good of others, strive to attain the results you want to achieve by implementing a plan of action. Visualize the positive results of your aspirations and the good that they will do for you and for mankind.

Meditation

At times you doubt your abilities, but it is not inability but doubt that holds you back. You are in charge of your life at this very moment! Everything that is good and kind will unfold with the help of your deep and abiding conviction.

Self-judgment

Reverse the power of past judgment by emptying your mind of any negative thoughts that may be controlling you. This does not mean living in denial or oblivion; it means releasing the negative energy that causes you to condemn your self. Emptying your mind is a major step toward taking control over how you wish to think.

Meditation

Releasing negative thoughts takes work and repetition. As long as it is not destructive to yourself or others, there are many ways to let go of negative energy. A wonderful form of release is to write your feelings on paper, read them so that you actually "see" and "hear" what you feel, and then throw the paper away. Once these feelings are recognized, they are no longer important.

Helplessness

There are times when the feelings of helplessness we sometimes experience are so overwhelming it seems there is never going to be any light at the end of the tunnel. The pain hurts so much that we begin to question whether it is worth the struggle; when this happens, we loose sight of the one ingredient that keeps us holding on—our worthiness.

Meditation

No matter how dismal life gets at this moment, believe that the love of the universe is your gift; accept it with graciousness and open arms.

Dependency can evoke rage

Learned helplessness and loss of self-esteem derive from the inability to love our self. We turn outward, finding faulty relationships to fill the emptiness that is continually haunting us. Various unhealthy relationships fill the void for a while, until the disappointment and rage can no longer be repressed and escalate to reinforce our sense of inadequacy and powerlessness. Our dependency on others to fill us with love will only cause perpetual dependency instead of interdependency, which is really what we are striving for.

Meditation

If you are in a relationship that is not allowing you to grow and be at peace, maybe it is time to take stock and look at what is keeping you in a dead-end situation. Know with deep conviction that you deserve to be with someone with whom you can shine.

Failure

Our experiences in life are lessons from which we can learn. The lessons are not meant to make us feel defeated, but to strengthen us. Failures are not inadequacies by which to evaluate one's self. Those who choose to succeed have had failures; the only difference is that they never give up. Most of all, they use their shortfalls as a driving force to succeed and make their dreams come true; they never, ever, base their self-worth on failure.

Meditation

Right now, see that nothing that has brought you down has any power over you, either at this very moment or in the future. Affirm that everything that has been, is no more. Everything that will be, shall be as you wish. All that was given was a gift by which to become stronger and wiser. Use the gift as it was meant to be used.

Addictions

Addictions are habitual acts that separate us from ourselves and reality. Addictions are used to escape seemingly inescapable despair, guilt, shame and pain, immobilizing and imprisoning us. Anything that detaches us from our feelings and thoughts can be very soothing for the moment, until reality demands that we face up to and deal with the problem. Addictions cause us to block out the problem at hand, thus controlling our ability to address the underlying causes. Be determined to see the problem face on, and to work toward a solution that will remove whatever is stopping you from going forward in life.

Meditation

Believe, deeply and sincerely, that you can use your inner power instead of being powerless. This can only be done by affirming your right to happiness and disclaiming all negative thoughts that interfere with the truth that you are worthy. Slowly, if you recognize your own power, the addictive behaviour will fade into nothingness. The need to escape from yourself dissipates as you turn inward for strength and fortitude, to the only place where it can be found.

We can change our circumstances

When we feel we are unable to better our circumstances, uncertainty controls our minds and we become filled with doubt. This leads to loss of personal strength, and we tend to forget about the power of our inner creativity. We can acquire a sense of calm assurance by focusing on the certainty that we can change our destiny.

Meditation

Affirm,

I now choose to create a life for myself that is guided by the power of certainty. I am steadfast in my conviction that I am free to have control over what can be changed, in order to bring myself peace and joy.

Listen to the truth within

We see and hear what we want to see and hear, and we react according to what we have learned from our past experiences. If we close our eyes and quiet our mind's activity, there is a place within where peace exists. It is our own connection to truth, it is our perception that goes beyond all senses or intellect: it comes from our heart.

Meditation

To do this meditation it is advisable to be laying down in a quiet, dimly lit room. Get comfortable and breath slowly and deeply until your mind is relaxed. Do not let any thoughts come into your mind. Wait as long as it takes to clear your mind.

Once you are still, repeat,

I am free from all that can affect my peace of mind.
I am free to listen to my inner voice of truth.

Life is incomplete without love

We must make a solemn oath to love ourselves. Loving ourself does not mean we are self-centered. It means recognizing our inner beauty. We were born innocent and loving. Our core self has not changed, only the cloak we wear to protect ourselves. Take the cloak off and experience the child of joy that waits within. Embrace what truly is your right, accept the love that belongs to you.

Meditation

Find a picture of yourself when you were a child, somewhere between the ages of six months and five years old.

The child you see is beautiful, loving and perfect. You still are that same person now. Feel the joy that child represents. See how beautiful you really are.

It is natural to feel loss, but to do so to the degree that it causes debilitating despair is not natural. If a present event causes overwhelming despair, the pain of an unresolved past event may be the trigger. The intensity of anguish we sometimes feel is an accumulation of past disappointments that lurk in our subconscious, waiting to be healed. Every event is different, in that time and circumstances change how we deal with the event. If there is lack of understanding, there will be an inability to cope in a functional way. It is better to start at the beginning and work out lingering issues, than to try and go forward without being cleansed of the past.

Meditation

Look at past but similar circumstances—ones that cause the same feelings you experience in the present. If you are honest with yourself, you will see a correlation between present emotional responses and past events. The unresolved issues and feelings must be healed before you can look to the present with any degree of clarity.

Peaceful living is your gift

Have you ever sat quietly alone by the ocean or mountains and savored a splendid beauty and oneness with nature? The solitude that encompasses our being when we see and hear nature, is how our life should be. The more deeply we desire this peace, the more readily we are guided to the means by which to receive it. Peace and harmony are our true psychological state, which is attained by our willingness to get over past inflictions of shame, guilt and anger.

Meditation

I seek joy and forgiveness.
I seek harmony and peace today.

You are a winner

The power of our past habits is sometimes too hard to resist when we are trying to accomplish change. At the moment of indulgence, we forget ourselves and succumb to the moment of gratification.

Once we take a few steps toward loving ourselves and experiencing inner peace, we no longer need to run and hide behind unhealthy habits.

Meditation

I will not resign myself to anything that controls my well-being.

I will not allow anything from the past to control my inner happiness.

Becoming liberated

We do not have to forget what someone has done to us, we just need to forgive. Unless we forgive, our life will be filled with anger and pain.

Forgiving entails releasing, understanding and accepting.

Releasing means confronting the past experience, feeling what has to be felt, and letting go, for in so doing the past pain is released.

Understanding is the second stage that automatically follows releasing. The hurt is faced head-on so that the pain is washed away from our sub-conscious, leaving us free to go on.

Accepting what happened is the final stage. The past happened, it was beyond our control; therefore, it has no impact on the beginning of our liberation.

Meditation

I release all past mistakes from my subconscious.

Forgiving is my grace, and I no longer hold myself or others in contempt, for all that has been cannot affect the present.

Peace starts in our hearts

Peace comes to those who seek it and give it. Peace comes to those who know where and how to find it. Peace starts in our hearts, but first we must be free of fear and anger. The residue of a tainted past prevents us from experiencing peaceful thoughts, because unconsciously our hearts are pleading with us to release the pain. Unless we desire to change how we view the past, it will haunt us, preventing our happiness in the present.

Meditation

I no longer choose to allow the past to be a roadblock to my development as a whole and happy person. Peace is my right and my goal.

Cleansing our life

If we wash our hands and they are cleansed by water, we can also wash away our troubles and pain. Tears are a means of cleansing our distraught heart, thereby releasing the sorrow from inside our body. Once the pain is released, there is an insight that prevails and guides us to peace. There is a renewing of our spirit and refreshing of our life.

Meditation

Do not be afraid to cleanse your heart by weeping; that is what tears are for. Wash away the pain that tortures your soul. Release the memories that hold you back from being cleansed and free.

Repeat,

My tears wash away the memory that has caused me sorrow.

I am not afraid to weep and release my anger and hurt.

I really believe that things will be brighter.

Why did it happen?

At times it is difficult to understand why we were a victim of someone else's sickness. The victim suffers the results of the violator's obsessions, and it is the victim who bears the burden of having to repair the damage.

But, it is also the victim who becomes victorious and compassionate and who is ultimately rewarded. It is the victim who heals, who understands that which is at times hard to understand. It is the victim who helps others believe that they, too, will heal from the abuse of others.

Meditation

Glory and peace be mine!

A major step

Once you begin to heal, you will gain control over your life, instead of fearing the power of that which controls you. Healing washes away fears that subconsciously prevent you from being in control of yourself and your destiny. A sense of helplessness will no longer paralyse your power to do what you want with your life. You will feel inspired by your newly found strength.

Meditation

I release all hate, resentment and fear from my being.

I release all that controls my ability to make decisions that are right for me.

I release all that causes obsessions and addictions. Hurt can no longer keep me down.

I am free to make the decisions that will naturally bring me joy.

Maturity versus immaturity

There are three transitional learning stages on the way to becoming a whole person. They are childhood, adulthood, and selfhood—the ultimate stage where we experience autonomy, happiness and peace of mind. Unfortunately, we are not guided through the stages to selfhood, so we must take into our own hands the responsibility for completing this process. Unless we have worked out our childhood feelings and unhealthy past, the transition from adulthood to selfhood is a rocky one. Until we take the responsibility for claiming selfhood, we will be tarnished with the remnants of unhealthy attitudes, behaviours and actions with ourselves and others.

Meditation

I am firm in my conviction that I must work out the unresolved feelings that keep me from being a whole and fulfilled person.

I am willing to grow and be all that I am capable of being.

I am moving forward on my journey to self-discovery.

Stuck in pain

Events that cause us emotional pain can create lingering memories if the pain itself is not released. Although we are unable to change the past, we do have the power to change how we view the past. If we carefully release a memory from our subconscious, look at the pain it causes without the clutter of "if only," we break through to another depth of understanding. In other words, we become free of the control that pain exerts on our life. We become liberated from repeating the same scenarios and patterns.

Meditation

Life offers gifts of understanding and freedom.
I welcome them into my life!

Seeking outward approval

Do you sell your soul for the sake of approval? Do you feel a deep longing for love but are unable to feel it from within yourself? If so, life is not very rewarding, for all your energy is spent on satisfying the whims of others because you need their acceptance. This leaves a deep, undeniably empty space. There is an alternative, of course; it is to know love within your self, instead of trying to gain approval from others.

Inner love nourishes your being with joy and peace that radiate to the world outside. Your inner self is where true sanctuary is found. It is the only place where lasting satisfaction resides.

Meditation

You will need to put time aside to be alone and quiet your thoughts to hear the voice that waits to be heard. You will need to desire inner satisfaction deeply enough to let go of the need for outward approval.

I acknowledge that I do not accept myself, or I would not so desperately want the approval of others.

I now make the commitment to love and accept myself.

Everyone has the right to strive for happiness

Everlasting happiness can only be found through realization of its source. It is the extension of love. It is the natural joy one feels when there is harmony with the beauty of living. It is the right of every living being; it is attainable by desiring it with deep passion. There are, perhaps, times when that desire is strong enough to give us a brief glimpse of the treasures happiness bestows. Then the glory of what is bestowed guides us patiently home to where the comfort and healing take place. Home is right where we are at every moment; what is bestowed is right inside our very own heart, waiting for us.

Meditation

You have experienced a glimpse of ultimate joy at some moment in your life. Maybe it was the birth of a child, the solitude of the country, or ecstasy during love-making. The joy was felt deep within your heart.

I want to feel a constant oneness with my Creator.

Understanding control

There are two polarities of control—in control or out of control. Being in control gives us the power to live peacefully. Out of control, we cause everyone and everything to exist in a very unstable fashion. Being out of control causes everything outside ourselves to affect our well-being, so we live in a reactionary state.

Even in nature, there is an order that keeps the universe from destroying itself and everything around it. It is the order of natural control. When there is any deviation from nature's law of order, chaos erupts. Harmonious control is not forceful, it proceeds naturally, understanding what will be needed to make life peaceful.

Meditation

From this moment on, I choose to be in a natural, quiet state of control.

Changing ineffective patterns

Ineffective patterns are not hard to change, once you become aware of the ill effects they are having on you. Take the time to look at the different aspects of your life that are preventing positive development. Recognize the power that ineffective attitudes and behaviours wield on your peace of mind. Ineffective behaviours evolve from repetitive reinforcement of negative events that have occurred in your life.

Meditation

I now see what is preventing my peace of mind.

I am taking charge of my life and accept the responsibility to make the changes I must make to be at peace.

It gets a little rocky at times

At times as we mend our lives, we feel the road is too rocky to go on. New emotions emerge, old ones take control, and then we feel helpless again. If we could only contain the fear and the overwhelming feeling of helplessness it would be so much easier. But, to do a job worthwhile, helplessness has to be recognized so that confidence can prevail. Emotions must be experienced, explored and understood, before the healing starts. Be patient; we have waited this long, and the results are worth it. There is a light at the end of the tunnel.

Meditation

At times it seems so difficult, but my reward will be confidence, and my dreams will come true.

Closeness

Is it hard to feel deeply connected to another person? Does it feel as if there is something missing in your personal relationships? If so, it is time to become closer to your own self. As close as you are to your own self is as close as you can possibly be to anyone else. If you keep your distance, are mistrustful or fear intimacy, these are issues that should be looked at and worked out within your own self. Only when you are connected to your own inner strength and love, can you connect to others harmoniously.

Meditation

For one day observe how much time is spent thinking about everything other than resolving your own personal issues. Then, in the evening, go to a quiet place and relax. Put aside all thoughts that pertain to anything other than your own personal issues that need to be looked at honestly. Then spend time being thoughtful, repeating loving kind messages to yourself. Replace each disturbing thought immediately with positive healing thoughts and words.

Within myself there is love that heals all that has been broken. I have been hurt in the past, but the scars will be erased so I may share my life, so that I may love and be loved.

Healing takes time

Unfortunately, healing does not happen overnight; there are no quick fixes for healing a life. The good days are great, the bad ones are not so great. There are moments we cannot even trust the calm that we feel. There are times when it all seems so useless, and we wonder why we should bother. Why? Because it is our right to be happy and enjoy the worthiness of our life. Also, it is our right to end our own struggles, be peaceful, and achieve what will make us happy.

It is our obligation to care for ourselves first, for we must do this before we can give proper care to anyone or anything else. Then, how we treat others will reflect the love and kindness with which we treat ourselves.

Meditation

Believe that it is your given right to be healed. Trust in the power of the universe to guide you. Trust that everything always works out, but most of all believe that you are of great importance.

Your choice... optimism or cynicism

There is never a risk if you adopt a cynical attitude, because there is no possibility of disappointment. All that is gained is a negative approach to life and fear of the unknown. The opposite to this attitude is optimism, which is assurance, acceptance and, most of all, understanding. Every rose that buds is optimistic that the sun will shine. Then it unfolds its inner beauty.

Meditation

Optimism is hope that everything will get better, for it always does.

Optimism is belief that everything will turn out for the best, and it always does!

Let go of that which does not belong to you

Most of us are not even aware of the guilt with which we burden ourselves. Guilt causes us to think defensively and blame others. No one is to blame for our outlook except us. We alone decide how we think and what we want.

So claim your right to take control of your thoughts and destiny. Let go of guilt and blame because they have no place in your life. When we take responsibility and stop blaming others, we set ourselves free from the inner turmoil that is caused by guilt. We then establish a positive connection within ourselves and with those around us.

Meditation

I will not claim unhealthy guilt as mine.

I will not blame anyone else for how I feel.

My thoughts are my own, and I have the right to believe in myself.

Slowly all the hurt fades away, and joy replaces the emptiness

A time will come when everything that used to be confusing becomes clear. A time will come when you pack all your past hurts and disappointments into a bundle, and observe them from a distance. You will become the "viewer" of this information; it will be stored as your resource centre, for quick reference. It is a place from which you can draw information, to use in dealing with new situations. As the viewer, you will no longer be the reactor, you will be free to become centered on your own, independent, healthy thoughts.

Meditation

This is a wonderful meditation; you can actually visualize your life being mended.

See your life in the palm of your hand. This is your journey, make it wholesome, make it a celebration and victory.

Repeat,

I am committed to honoring and loving myself and the life I create.

Healthy relationships

Healthy relationships are based on the positive energy that is shared and received by both participants. Both participants maintain an understanding and respect for each other's positive attributes. As individuals, they build on the positive in themselves and each other. They learn to understand the not-so-positive, and help each other to deal with it, or change if they so wish. This allows them to share more of themselves, because there are no reasons to *defend* their uniqueness. There is mutual acceptance.

Meditation

By recognizing the uniqueness of ourselves and others we enhance the world in which we live.

I have so much to offer and contribute to others because I am giving from my heart.

I have so much to discover in the world I create for myself and others.

Love who you are

A positive relationship starts with yourself first. If you see yourself as uncaring, unhappy and unfulfilled, you will create that reality. If you believe that you can change unhappiness into happiness, you will. The change starts as you focus on your positive qualities. Appreciate yourself, not for what you have, but for who you are. You are a unique individual with unique gifts to offer. Even your shortcomings are part of you, so accept them until they are corrected. Learn to love, honour and accept *the whole package*.

Meditation

Today I will focus on and share my positive self.

Today and everyday I will revitalise my being with passion and energy.

Today and everyday I will watch the natural changes that take place as I learn to accept myself.

The power of believing in yourself

If you do not believe in yourself, how do you expect anyone else to?

So fill your mind with good thoughts and they will be in your everyday life. Fill your mind with positive dreams, and they will come true. Focus on your uniqueness, and let it guide you as you develop your creative gifts. Define with conviction where you want to be in life. Fill your mind with the awareness of your own inner power that brings immense self-acceptance and self-love.

Goal

Attaining what will make you happy!

Step One

Recognize what will make you happy. Identify what is preventing you from reaching your goals, deal with the problem and let it go. Likely all that is preventing you from taking the appropriate steps you must take is fear. *There is nothing to be afraid of.*

The most important aspect of making your dream reality is the depth of your passion for the dream.

Meditation

Focus on what will make you happy. Take a piece of paper and write down the steps toward achieving an important objective. Make sure it is a reasonable goal, though. Now take the first step and practice it until you can go on to the next step. By the time all steps are repeated the goal will be accomplished. Remember, one step at a time.

Courage

It takes passion, fortitude and, most of all, courage to master life. Without courage we live, but do not know life. Courage comes from really believing that our contribution to life is very important. Courage frees us to venture into life, rather than hide away from it. The more we understand courage, the more we are able to grow!

Meditation

Courage is believing in our convictions and going beyond simple belief.

Today I will think only of courage, as I know that the opposite is fear.

Problems do not go away, they only get resolved

The only way to solve problems is to confront them at the very onset and work them out completely. Effective solutions cannot take place unless the time is taken to clearly evaluate the situation. Solving problems does not mean ignoring them or finding hasty solutions; it means seeing them clearly and finding the appropriate remedy. If problems are not resolved in a timely fashion with a healthy outcome, they become too painful and difficult to solve.

Meditation

To start, tackle the smallest problem facing you. Think only about finding a solution. To do this more easily, write down the problem so that it becomes more visible to you. This also makes it more objective. On one side of the paper, write the solutions that will be fair and will bring the best result. On the other side of the paper write down the likely outcome if a solution is not found.

Affirm,

I know that the solution already exists.
It is there, waiting for me to find.

Trust

If we do not have trust we are disconnected from living, and our energy is depleted guarding us from possible pain. We cheat ourselves by not allowing ourselves the freedom of giving and receiving. In the long run, if we do not heal, we are left with bitterness and an inability to love. If we operate from this narrow framework that no one is to be trusted, we end up in situations that confirm our fragmented belief system.

To transcend these limitations we must first come to terms with what has caused us to be so bitter. And we must believe that there are those whom we can trust. This is vital if we are to move beyond doubt and fear. If we do not heal, we miss what really counts in life: the expression of love.

Meditation

For one moment, I want to feel the joy of being able to trust.

Then trust is what I seek to bestow upon myself.

Love must be cultivated to flourish

Love multiplies as it flows, enriching even the most distant of observers. To share and give love we must know the completeness of love. Love is knowing the importance of others as we know our own meaningfulness.

Love does not seek gain from its recipient. Love's genuine purpose is to multiply and bring joy.

As time and eternity are inseparable, so love and life are inseparable.

Meditation

Love is my gift and my right. I give to myself this wholesome way of thinking so that I may share with others.

Positive energy

Positive energy heals. The universe has given us an immense capacity for life-sustaining energy. We can heal our hearts, souls and bodies by connecting to the power within our own beings. It is a power that can move mountains. Positive energy is the creative force of life from God. The birds sing in celebration and rejoice in its beauty.

Meditation

Anger and resentment are negative blocks that prevent the power of love from healing us. The blocks must be dissipated so that positive energy can synchronize our minds, bodies and souls back to their original harmonious state.

Make the choice

You can be successful and happy! You create what you want from life. Decide what you really want and where you want to go. Do what you have to do in order to get there, think about what can and will be, not about what was. You are a contributor and a participator in life. So live the life you want and let go of what was. No one will do it for you, so you must take charge. This is your life. Make it happen!

Meditation

This is now, with a new beginning. No matter what your station in life has been until now, you can change your mind about where you want to go. Now is the time to make it happen.

This is my life, I am in control of where I am and where I want to go.

Once more,

This is my life, I am in control of where I am and where I want to go.

And again,

This is my life, I am in control of where I am and where I want to go.